A. da Silva Costa Junior
Rubenia Costa
Aline Ferreira

Outsourcing in Labour Relations in Brazil

A. da Silva Costa Junior
Rubenia Costa
Aline Ferreira

Outsourcing in Labour Relations in Brazil

The Main Problems of Labour Outsourcing in the Legal World

ScienciaScripts

Imprint
Any brand names and product names mentioned in this book are subject to trademark, brand or patent protection and are trademarks or registered trademarks of their respective holders. The use of brand names, product names, common names, trade names, product descriptions etc. even without a particular marking in this work is in no way to be construed to mean that such names may be regarded as unrestricted in respect of trademark and brand protection legislation and could thus be used by anyone.

Cover image: www.ingimage.com

This book is a translation from the original published under ISBN 978-3-330-75987-9.

Publisher:
Sciencia Scripts
is a trademark of
Dodo Books Indian Ocean Ltd. and OmniScriptum S.R.L publishing group

120 High Road, East Finchley, London, N2 9ED, United Kingdom
Str. Armeneasca 28/1, office 1, Chisinau MD-2012, Republic of Moldova, Europe
Printed at: see last page
ISBN: 978-620-8-07907-9

SUMMARY

The main objective of this work is to identify conceptual and legal aspects of outsourcing in the relevant literature, by means of a bibliographical survey, as well as to describe the guiding principles of labor law, which guarantee the rights of outsourced workers. It also aims to identify the main weaknesses in the legislation pertaining to outsourcing. As is well known, outsourcing is a practice that is being used more and more in companies. Thus, studying the legal aspects related to the practice of outsourcing is of great importance, given the relevance of the subject. In this paper, considerations were raised about the evolution of Labor Law, as a way of underpinning this study. This is followed by a brief history of outsourcing, among other related issues of significant importance. This paper also discusses Bill 4.330/2004, a controversial but necessary bill for the regulation of outsourcing. This topic was chosen as a result of the author's experience in an extracurricular internship in the labor area, actively participating in hearings in the various labor courts in the states of Paraiba, Pernambuco and Rio Grande do Norte, regarding the support of outsourced workers in banks, who performed the company's core business. According to the study's findings, illicit outsourcing, the main focus of this work, is becoming increasingly common in the Brazilian economy and despite various discussions between workers, trade unions, trade unions and government officials, no solution has yet been found.

Key words: Outsourcing. Workers. Legal norms.

SUMMARY

Chapter 1	**7**
Chapter 2	**11**
Chapter 3	**22**
Chapter 4	**25**
Chapter 5	**39**
Chapter 6	**42**

INTRODUCTION

One of the fastest growing forms of contracting in Brazil is the outsourcing of labor. Its main objective is not only to optimize services, but to maximize profits to the detriment of reducing labor and social security charges, which is why there has been a lot of discussion on this subject.

The growth of outsourcing in the private sector is not only occurring in Brazil, it is a practice that has been used in many countries, in those considered to be first world countries, such as the United States of America, as well as in European countries and also in developing countries such as Brazil. The growth of this form of labor contracting and the transfer of certain activities from the service provider is primarily due to the increase in company profits.

According to the understanding and concept of Garcia (2008, p. 305), outsourcing is "the transfer of certain peripheral activities of the service taker, to be carried out by different and specialized companies".

There is a need for companies to create alternatives that are effective and that aim to reduce the difficulties of business continuity in our country. It is therefore necessary for organizations to create and develop sustainable development mechanisms, with the aim of reducing expenses, i.e. costs, in order to maximize profits and guarantee their permanence in today's highly competitive market.

In this neoliberal capitalist system that prevails in the market, whether national or international, companies have no choice but to adapt to the demands of this market, bearing in mind that today, competitiveness is increasing and so are consumer demands, because today consumer demands for price and product quality are much higher.

Therefore, all the effort that organizations put in is aimed at achieving goals and making more profit. Outsourcing is therefore a way of achieving these goals, because in this way the company reduces its expenses with salaries, holidays, 13th salary, sick leave, etc.

The outsourcing of labor began in the 1940s, during the Second World War, in the United States, when the war industry began to request certain types of support activities from other companies, leaving only those they considered to be the main ones. This process came to be known in management as *Dowsizing* (reconcentration of companies) or *outsourcing* (de-verticalization).

These, then, were the first steps taken towards the emergence of outsourcing, which today is increasingly used by companies in general. The aim of outsourcing is to reduce costs and thus, as a natural consequence, increase the profits of organizations, as already mentioned. It therefore aims to reduce production costs and improve the economy. In fact, outsourcing seeks to improve quality, competitiveness and productivity, all of which are essential for any company, given the increasing competitiveness of the national and international business scene.

On the other hand, we should not underestimate the existence of some negative effects of this process that could harm workers, such as: the reduction in the number of vacancies, the reduction of staff, the reduction of salaries, the cutting of benefits, employee dissatisfaction, among many others.

In Brazil, outsourcing began to be implemented by the automobile industry, under the name "third-party service contracting". At that time, the term outsourcing was not yet used.

In recent years, outsourcing has been used more and more, causing concern for workers and society. Not least for labor law scholars and the labor judiciary. The institute has been used abusively, without due respect for legal regulations and without adequate supervision.

Everyone's concern about the possible damage it could cause to workers is justified by the fact that there is still no clear and 100 percent effective legislation to deal with outsourcing.

Meanwhile, for company managers, it's better to recommend and encourage outsourcing as a way for companies to become more competitive and profitable. Of course, the main thing for companies is the profits they can make, while the workers, their collaborators, are, as a rule, treated as a handmaiden to their enterprises.

According to Giosa (2003, p.84):

> Hiring third-party services will lead to advantages for the company in terms of lower operating costs, compared to the costs practiced when the services were in-house; there will be greater profitability and growth for companies, with the reinforcement of their activities in the company's core business, which will be stimulated to fulfill its mission.

Notwithstanding these advantages, there are factors that are restrictive, such as: the lack of knowledge of the labor legislation specific to this case, as well as the probable establishment of conflict with the unions, i.e. showing that a good number of companies are still not properly equipped to deal with outsourcing in the right way. They see outsourcing only through the prism of profit, without worrying about the most important part of this relationship: the workers - their daily collaborators.

Both the government and the private sector can only outsource a service in cases where it is a middle activity, i.e. an activity that does not represent its main purpose. This is possible both for the production of goods and for the provision of services, such as cleaning, surveillance and so on.

However, in practice this is not the case, mainly due to the existence of a large number of companies that distort the purpose of this institute, creating a precarious and unfair employment relationship in order to take advantage.

Delgado (2008, p. 432) cites in his work Curso de Direito do Trabalho:

> The labor law operator lacks the necessary tools to overcome the perplexity and submit the socio-legal process of outsourcing to the essential guidelines of Labor Law, so as not to allow it to become the antithesis of the principles, institutes and rules that have always been the civilizing and distinctive mark of this legal branch in the context of Western culture.")

Emphasizing the above reasoning, the author Catharino (1997, p.71) calls outsourcing a sequel to neoliberalism and goes on to add:

> For this reason, and for all the rest that could be said, outsourcing is a way of ultimately exploiting human labor, which is basically considered a commodity, as pure economists like the neoliberals, who advocate the maximum liberalization of a self-regulating market, like to do.

Outsourcing is therefore advantageous for the neo-liberal capitalist system, which sees the worker not as a human being in the first place, but as a cog in the company's wheel, who can be replaced at any time by one that offers more financial advantages.

The question therefore arises as to whether the use of labor outsourcing is lawful, with the hypothesis that it is possible to use the institute, but only in its legal form, which in practice has not been as effective as expected. However, we have to understand that outsourcing is a practice that is increasingly being adopted by companies and that there is no going back from this, so there must be laws for this.

This topic was chosen because of the author's experience in an extracurricular internship in the labor area, actively participating in hearings in the various labor courts in the state of Paraiba, relating to claims by outsourced workers in banks, who performed the company's core business. The methodology used to prepare this monograph is bibliographical research, carried out in books and electronic articles of recognized scientific quality.

1. CONSIDERATIONS ON THE EVOLUTION OF LABOR LAW IN BRAZIL

Labor law is relatively new. While work is as old as the very existence of man. From the beginning of man's history, as far as we know, he has naturally been obliged to work, out of the need to satisfy his hunger and guarantee his self-defense. Fishing, cloaking and fighting dangerous animals as well as his fellow man are basic, primitive human occupations for survival. Over time, the barter system and the exploitation of other people's labor began.

According to Nascimento (2004, p.79):

> History records the existence of slave labor as far back as 4000 B.C. - the practice of the "objectification" of the working man. As early as the Middle Ages, there were the following basic types of workers: 1) vassals, subjugated by contract to the feudal lord; 2) serfs of the soil, almost slaves, who could even be sold, given away or exchanged for other serfs and/or goods and; 3) craftsmen, who worked for themselves and sold their goods.

Slowly, workers gained better conditions, even if their basic rights were still not respected. At the end of the Middle Ages, however, something similar to contemporary trade unionism began to emerge: organizations representing products and workers. Both faced each other in defense of their opposing rights, thus giving rise to the class struggle (NASCIMENTO, 2004).

With the Industrial Revolution in the 18th century, labor law emerged, perhaps motivated by the social pressure resulting from the discovery of machinery as a substitute for workers' strength, which increased unemployment and, consequently, further exploitation of the unemployed workforce.

According to Delgado (2009, p.59) the phases of Labor Law are as follows:

> 1 - *Formation* - extends from 1802 to 1848, with its initial moment in the *Peel's Act of* the early nineteenth century in England, which basically deals with protective rules for minors, this English law aimed to set certain restrictions on the use of child labor. The laws of this phase were basically aimed at reducing the brutal violence of corporate overexploitation of women and minors. These laws were humanitarian in nature, with an unsystematic approach. The labor law spectrum is still dispersed, without creating its own autonomous legal branch.
>
> 2 - *Intensification* - between 1848 and 1890, with the initial milestones being the *"Communist Manifesto of 1848"* and, in France, the results of the 1848 Revolution, such as the establishment of freedom of association and the creation of the Ministry of Labor.
> 3 - *Consolidation* - from 1890 to 1919. Its initial milestones are the Berlin Conference (1890) and the Catholic Encyclical *Rerum Novarum* (1891) - Pope Leo XIII. This Encyclical made ample reference to the need for a new attitude on the part of the ruling classes towards the so-called "Social Question", which included in its text the obligations of employers and

> employees, emphasizing the respect and dignity of the working class, both spiritually and physically, on the other hand, the worker should faithfully comply with what he had contracted; never use violence in his demands, or use artificial means to achieve his objectives.
> 4 - The *autonomy of* labor law began in 1919 and lasted throughout the decades of the 20th century. Its initial frontiers were marked by the creation of the ILO (1919) and the constitutions of Mexico (1917) and Germany (1919) (DELGADO, 2009).

According to the aforementioned author, soon after the end of the First World War, the so-called *social constitutionalism* emerged - the inclusion in the constitutions of provisions concerning the protection of social interests, including guaranteeing labor rights. The first constitution to provide for labor law was that of Mexico in 1917.

According to Nascimento (2004, p.47):

> In 1927, Italy, concerned about the situation of its workers, drew up the *Carta Del Lavoro,* which established a corporatist system and served as an inspiration for other political systems, such as Portugal, Spain and Brazil. In corporatism, the aim was to organize the entire economy and society around the state, promoting the so-called national interest by interfering in and regulating all aspects of relations between people. In this model, the unions had no autonomy, and union organization was tied to the state.

In this context, the Universal Declaration of Human Rights of 1948 provides for various labor rights, such as limits on working hours, paid holidays, among others.

According to Martins (2012, p.654):

> In Brazil, the first federal constitution to deal with labor rights in a transparent manner was that of 1934, influenced by social constitutionalism. It provided various guarantees for workers, such as protection for women's work, an 8-hour working day, etc. The 1937 Constitution marked a phase of state intervention in labor law and other areas; it created a single union linked to the state, to exercise delegated functions of public power, established the normative competence of each labor court, among others. In addition, there were countless rules dealing with labour rights, and the need arose to organize them. Thus, in 1943, the CLT was approved. As time went by, new laws emerged, such as the Law on Domestic Workers, the Law on Temporary Workers, the Law on Paid Weekly Rest, the Law establishing the 13th Salary, etc. The 1964 and 1967 Constitutions maintained the workers' rights provided for in the previous Constitutions, as well as including other rights; and in 1988 the current Constitution was approved, dealing with labor rights from Articles 7 to 11.

It should also be remembered that Human Rights, when dealing with Social Fundamental Rights expressed in art. 6 of the 1988 Federal Constitution, considering that their emergence complements what is recommended in the 1948 Declaration. The right to work is of the utmost importance to citizens, as it dignifies them and makes them important to society.

According to Delgado (2009, p. 97):

> Social rights were born out of a historical moment in which the imbalance between the living conditions of different social classes served to foster the idea that the individual could turn to the government and receive guarantees from it, or rather, state services. It is worth pointing out that social rights, especially the right to work, are essential, unassailable and therefore fundamental rights.

The right to work requires the state to take an active role. In this way, the individual has the right to demand guarantees from the government in order to improve their living conditions. Article 6 of the Federal Constitution of 1988 sets out various social rights, including the right to work.

According to Montal (2010, p.115):

> Work represents a form of "invisible link" between the individual and the state, stemming from the feeling of belonging to the same legal category, a feeling of fraternity that unites the members of a society. In this respect, professional *status* is loaded with social significance, so that anyone who is not included in the "world of work" is practically excluded from society.

Therefore, the right to work, when materialized through work itself, brings social justice and inclusion, promoting peace and balance in social relations, dignifying the worker, so that he or she feels important and useful to society.

In short, labor law has evolved a lot in the last few decades of the 20th century, and today workers are protected by the Federal Constitution and by specific, modern laws. Even so, there is still room for improvement in labor law, which is dynamic and therefore keeps pace with social evolution and change, which is its main purpose. And it is in this context that, due to the phenomenon of globalization, which has intensified the competitiveness of companies so that they can cope with the demands of the present, alternatives to new labour relations often arise, as is the case with outsourcing, the subject of this work.

Thus, in a preliminary way, outsourcing, according to Oliveira (2012, p.21):

> It has many and varied definitions. For some who are comfortable with the phenomenon, they point to its dissemination, and claim that outsourcing is the "horizontalization of economic activity, according to which many large companies are transferring to others part of the functions they had previously carried out directly, progressively concentrating on an increasingly restricted list of activities.

The term "outsourcing" should be understood as an administrative technique for decentralizing production, which culminates in a trilateral legal relationship in which the worker provides services to a service provider, despite having an employment contract with an intermediary or supplier company. It is therefore necessary to understand how outsourcing came about.

2. PRINCIPLES OF THE DIGNITY OF THE HUMAN PERSON

First of all, it is necessary to understand what the principle of human dignity is from the point of view of the philosopher Immanuel Kant (2007, p.68):

> Dignity is the value of everything that has no nail, i.e. cannot be replaced by an equivalent. In this way, dignity is a quality inherent to human beings as moral beings: to the extent that they exercise their practical reason autonomously, human beings construct distinct human personalities, each of which is absolutely individual and irreplaceable. Consequently, dignity is totally inseparable from autonomy in the exercise of practical reason, which is why only human beings have dignity.

It is worth noting that dignity is not only recognized by the law, but to the extent that the law recognizes it. However, it must not be forgotten that the law can play an indispensable role in its protection and promotion, so it is not completely without foundation that even the need for a legal concept of the dignity of the human person has been upheld, given that it is the proper value, that is, the nature of the human being.

Therefore, in accordance with the provisions of the UN Universal Declaration, as well as considering the understandings correlated in a demonstrative way, where it is observed that the core element of the notion of the dignity of the human person seems to continue to be reaffirmed, as well as the majority doctrine and especially Kantian, therefore focusing on the autonomy and the right of self-determination of the person.

Dignity is a quality inherent to human beings as moral beings, insofar as they exercise their practical reason autonomously, human beings construct distinct human personalities, each of which is exclusively individual and irreplaceable.

Thus, dignity is totally inseparable from autonomy to exercise practical reason, and it is because this is the case that only human beings have dignity.
According to Cunha (2008, p.85):

> The great legacy of Kantian thought for the philosophy of human rights, however, is equality in the attribution of dignity. To the extent that freedom in the exercise of practical reason is the only requirement for an entity to have dignity, and that all human beings enjoy this autonomy, it follows that the human condition is the necessary and sufficient factual support for dignity, regardless of any type of social recognition.

According to Comparato (2001, p. 76):

> The dignity of the person does not only consist in the fact that, unlike things, they are considered and treated as an end in themselves and never as a

> means to a certain end. It also results from the fact that, through his rational will, only the person lives in conditions of autonomy, that is, as a being capable of being guided by the laws that he himself enacts.

The dignity of the human person presupposes that the individual who possesses it is a free being, with individual and irreplaceable characteristics, and for these reasons this dignity is guaranteed by the Federal Constitution of 1988, and recognized by international treaties, such as the Treaty of Versailles - 1919, which created the International Labor Organization - ILO, as well as the Universal Declaration of Human Rights, in 1948, which recognizes in its 1st article that: "All men are born free and equal in dignity and rights. They are endowed with reason and conscience and should act towards one another in a spirit of brotherhood".

As you can see, in order to conceptualize the dignity of the human person, ideas, subjectivity, philosophy, among others, are used.

According to Cordeiro (2012, p.63):

> It does not have a concept made up of strictly objective content, as in some legal systems, but it does have a minimum of objectivity, in order to preserve legal certainty and to serve as a basis for theses with opposing directions, but its definition is established in a subjective way, because it has philosophical, ethical, anthropological and political influences. It is also grounded in the law and in the cultural values of each locality or society. The right to the dignity of the human person has religious and philosophical foundations. In religion, there is a foundation that we are constituted by God's love, which is the essence of this feeling, and because we are his image and likeness, because we are God's beloved children, and that we must share this divine love not only with our friends, but with all human beings. However, in philosophy, an important and indispensable feeling is contemplated, which is the "will", which is only found in people who are considered rational, capable of recognizing and adopting in their lives and in their relationships with others, conduct that is not the least essential for living together in a dignified manner.

Thus, there are various concepts of the dignity of the human person. The religious concept of the dignity of the human person has exerted a great deal of influence on the formation of the concept from the point of view of the law, followed by the philosophical foundations of the dignity of the human person.

According to Morais (2003, p.123):

> The principle of the dignity of the human person is a spiritual and moral value inherent to the person, which manifests itself uniquely in the conscious and responsible self-determination of one's own life and which brings with it a claim to respect from other people.

It is therefore imperative that human beings are treated with respect, consideration and equality, in line with the Federal Constitution, which states that everyone is equal before the law.

According to Cordeiro (2012, p.85):

> The Principle of the Dignity of the Human Person actually states what "respect for others" is, that is, what is ethical and moral so that human beings can have a social existence based on harmony, justice and the legitimization of rights that guarantee peaceful coexistence between citizens.

The dignity of the human person is listed in the Federal Constitution of 1988, making them fundamental values in the Brazilian legal system, thus giving values such as equality, fraternity, freedom, security and property.

Art. 1 The Federative Republic of Brazil, formed by the indissoluble un on of States and Municipalities and the Federal District, is a Democratic State governed by the rule of law and has as its foundations:

I sovereignty;

II citizenship;

III the dignity of the human person;

IV The social values of work and free enterprise.

It is understood that the concept of the dignity of the human person is in its simplest essence, however, extremely complex, developed in a diversity of values existing in society.

According to Sarlet (2007, p.62) when conceptualizing the dignity of the human person:

> The dignity of the human person is the intrinsic and distinctive quality of each human being that makes them deserving of the same respect and consideration by the State and the community, implying, in this sense, a complex of fundamental rights and duties that ensure the person against all acts of a degrading and inhuman nature, as well as guaranteeing them the minimum existential conditions for a healthy life, in addition to providing and promoting their active and co-responsible participation in the destinies of their own existence and life in communion with other human beings.

These constitutional guarantees can be seen in Article 5 of the Charter, which preserves the protective system of freedom as a way of making individual rights a reality, and the judiciary must be the instrument for defending fundamental rights, protecting citizens from the arbitrary excesses of the state.

Human rights arose over time out of the need to protect physical and psychological characteristics, as Norberto Bobbio (1992, p.5) states:

> Human rights, however fundamental they may be, are historical rights, in other words, born in certain circumstances, characterized by struggles to defend new freedoms against old powers, and born gradually, not all at once

and not all at once.

Since human dignity received constitutional protection, any abuse of the person has become unacceptable, no matter how small the violation. Unfortunately, however, these rights are still being violated today.

The 1988 Federal Constitution is the great legal milestone for human rights in Brazil. It brought substantive changes from the point of view of human rights in relation to the country's constitutional history, which seems to have been a natural consequence of the historical context experienced by the Constituent Assembly, which had the task of overcoming the regime of exception that had lasted for almost twenty years, while also ensuring fundamental rights.

According to Paulo and Alexandrino (2014, p. 37): The characteristics of fundamental rights are:

> • Imprescriptibility (fundamental rights do not disappear by course of time);
> • Inalienability (there is no possibility of transferring the rights fundamental to others);
> • Irrevocability (as a rule, fundamental rights cannot be renounced) object of the waiver);
> • Inviolability (impossibility of its non-observance by infra-constitutional provisions or by acts of public authorities);
> • Universality (must cover all individuals, regardless of their nationality, sex, race, creed or political-philosophical conviction);
> • Interdependence (the various constitutional provisions, although The freedom of movement is closely linked to the guarantee of *habeas corpus*, as well as the provision for imprisonment only in flagrante delicto or by order of the judicial authority);
> • Complementarity (fundamental rights must not be mutually exclusive) interpreted in isolation, but rather as a whole in order to achieve the objectives set out by the constituent legislator);
> • Relativity or limitability (fundamental rights do not have absolute nature).

Article 1 of the Magna Carta, when listing the foundations of the Brazilian state, in item III, affirms the dignity of the human person, which would already be enough to bring about a real "change" from a legal point of view.

In Article III, when listing the fundamental objectives of the Brazilian state, the Constitution is concerned with affirming the dignity of the human person, since "all objectives are related to the pursuit of the dignity of the human person".

For Immanuel Kant *apud* Cunha (2008, p.69), a distinction is made between law and morality from a formal and non-material point of view, i.e. the distinction depends on the reason for obeying the legal or moral norm. In a moral act, it can only be the very idea of duty, even if it is directly a legal duty and only indirectly a moral duty. However, in the same legal act, the motivation for acting can be, in addition to the moral motive of fulfilling one's duty, that of repulsion to the penalty, whether it be pecuniary or corporal punishment.

Being free and rational, man is capable of imposing on himself rules of conduct, designated by ethics, which are valid for all rational beings who, as such, are ends in themselves and not means at the service of others. Therefore, the basic rule of moral conduct that man can prescribe for himself is that in everything he does, he should always treat himself and his fellow human beings as ends and never as means. Thus, when applied to legal and social convenience, this basic moral rule becomes a rule of natural law (KANT, 2007).

If man were truly ethical, moral and law-abiding, there would be no injustice against workers or crimes against others.
and exactly the opposite. Kant (2007, 0.102) states:

> Man's obedience to his own free and autonomous will is the essence of morality and natural law. For this conception, legal norms will be natural law if their obligation is cognizable by pure reason, independent of external law, or positive law if they depend on external law for their obligation. However, on this occasion, we must presuppose a natural law, of an ethical order, which justifies the authority of the legislator, that is, his right to oblige others by a simple decision of his will. This natural law, which is the principle of all law, derives from human freedom, recognized through the categorical moral imperative.

There is no way of talking about the historical roots of the principle of human dignity without mentioning Kant, especially from the point of view that the human being is an entity endowed with rational autonomy and should never be seen as an instrument for satisfying the interests of others. Dignity is therefore presented as an achievement of ethical and legal reason. Its concept, however, is not peaceful.
According to Kant (1980, p.138):

> Dignity is the ethical self-determination of the human being, and autonomy is the foundation of dignity. The autonomy of the will means that the human being is capable of self-determination and acting in accordance with legal rules, a quality found only in rational creatures, i.e. every rational being exists as an end in itself and not as a means for the imposition of arbitrary wills. In all its actions, both those directed at itself and those directed at other rational beings, it must always be considered simultaneously as an end.

Over time, fundamental rights have evolved as an imperative for the harmonious survival of society, where respect for others is a non-negotiable prerogative. The expansion of these values inherent in the dignity of the human person has always been demanded by society. However, it is known that inequality still prevails in society, and this is due to many factors, such as the way of life where capitalism and other ideologies favor individualism. Having is more important than being, and so social injustices continue to be practiced.

The original Constituent Assembly, by establishing the dignity of the human person as the foundation of the Republic and the Democratic State of Law of Brazil in Article 1, III of the CF/88, ratified the meaning, purpose and justification of the exercise of state power and of the state itself, so that its actions are aimed at the individual.

It is therefore necessary to reaffirm that the principle of the dignity of the human person is, in other words, the true normative force of the 1988 Federal Constitution, which, together with democratic principles, makes it possible to build a more just and supportive society.

The Federal Constitution of 1988 established a concept of a Democratic and Social State of Law, adopting the dignity of the human person as one of its foundations. "Dignity personified in the objectives pursued by the new order". (ROCHA; SANTIAGO, 2012, p. 209).

With the publication of the Federal Constitution of 1988, a phase of full organization of the democratic state in Brazil began, and the principle of the dignity of the human person was promoted in Article 1, item III, which is considered to be one of the fundamental principles of the Magna Carta, and which aims to protect the human being as a whole, safeguarding the protection of their moral and spiritual values.

Incredibly, even today there are still cases of slave labor in Brazil, which is a serious violation of the Federal Constitution and other national and international institutes that vehemently combat this practice. This is a violation of the fundamental principles and rights of labor and the dignity of the human person. Law No. 10.803 of December 11, 2013, establishes penalties for the crime typified therein and indicates the hypotheses in which a condition analogous to slavery is configured and Law No. 12.781 of January 10, 2013, which also prohibits the exploitation of slave labor and labor in degrading conditions. It also prohibits the exploitation of slave labor in degrading conditions.

Slave-like work is characterized when the employee is unable to break away from the employer, through fraud or violence, and is forced to work against his or her will, in inhumane working conditions, often risking his or her life.

As already mentioned, this form of inhumane labor violates the 1988

Federal Constitution and Brazilian labor laws. In this sense, the International Labor Organization (ILO) has shown interest in combating and eradicating this cruel practice. The International Labor Conference held in 1919 approved the following principles: freedom of association and effective recognition of the right to collective bargaining; elimination of all forms of forced labor; effective abolition of child labor; elimination of all forms of discrimination in employment or occupation (CUNHA, 2008).

The resolutions described above, which came out of the International Labour Conference in 1919, represent the minimum necessary to characterize the dignity of the human person in labour relations.

The dignity of the human person (art. 1, III) - this principle brings together the unanimity of fundamental human rights and guarantees expressed in the Federal Constitution of 1988, when it proclaims the dignity of the human person, it is enshrining an imperative of social justice, a *supreme constitutional value.* Thus, the primacy embodies the space of moral integrity of the human being, regardless of creed, race, color, origin or social *status*. The content of the vector is broad and powerful, involving *spiritual* values (freedom to be, think and create, etc.) and *material* values (minimum income, health, food, leisure, housing, education, etc.). Its fulfillment represents victory against intolerance, prejudice, social exclusion, ignorance and oppression.

According to Bulos (2011, p.497):

> The dignity of the human person is intrinsic to the human being and should not be limited to the employee, so that the proposed dignified work reaches all individuals. With the promulgation of the current Constitution of the Republic in 1988, Brazil established itself as a welfare state, concerned primarily with the consolidation of citizenship, democracy, social justice and the dignity of the human person. Thus, once inferred from the political and social scenario that guides Brazilian society today, the principle of human dignity is affirmed as a constitutional norm and, thus, as a beacon for the country's jurisdictional activity.

Infra-constitutional rules and constitutional principles must be interpreted from the perspective of the principle of human dignity, using, where appropriate, the principle of proportionality to make them fit reality, thus achieving justice.

Labor relations can never take place without due respect for the principle of human dignity. After all, everything must revolve around the well-being of the individual and not their exploitation.

According to Rocha and Santiago (2012, p.209):

> The 1988 Federal Constitution established a conception of a Democratic and

> Social State of Law, adopting the dignity of the human person as one of its foundations. Dignity personified in the objectives pursued by the new order. With the promulgation of the Federal Constitution of 1988 comes a period of full organization of the democratic state in the country and promotes the principle of the dignity of the human person in article 1, item III, which is reported as part of the fundamental principles of the Constitution.

According to Martins (2008, p.147): "slavery was the first form of labor, where the slave was considered only an object, without any rights, his duty was only: to work, to work, and to work". Thus, it can be inferred that slavery is an unspeakable affront to the dignity of the human person, in the context of constitutional law as well as the legal norms that govern labor law.

For Basile (2011, p.193):

> After the liberation of slaves in colonial Brazil (the Aurea Law) and the spread of free, salaried work, the first constitutional provision on social rights and protection of labor was registered (1891), embodied in the freedom of association, without arms. However, it was the European immigrants of the post-war period (from 1919) who brought the ideology of freedom and equality (equal to die, equal to live), influencing class movements and the creation of various labor standards.

Also according to Basile (2011, p.197), in 1930 Getulio Vargas created the Ministry of Labor, Industry and Commerce, and in the following years he issued several labor decrees protecting employees. The issue of work under similar conditions can be defined as slavery as the exercise of human labor in which the freedom of the worker is restricted in any way, and/or when the minimum rights for the protection of the dignity of the worker are not respected. In short, the human being must be treated as a person, subject to dignity, regardless of any other born or acquired characteristic (OLIVEIRA, 2003, p.56).

2.1 THE PRINCIPLE OF HUMAN DIGNITY IN LABOR LAW

Labor law is based on respect for the dignity of the human person, respect for them and recognition of their value, regulating the relationship between employees and employers and ensuring that this relationship is as fair as possible.

According to Delgado (2011, p.50): "Labor Law is the instrument created to regulate the relationships between employees and employers so that these occur in a way that does not infringe any rights assisted to the worker".

The basic guideline of Labor Law is the protection of the worker, since the employee does not have the same legal equality as the employer, as happens with contractors in Civil Law. The purpose of labor law is to achieve true substantial equality between the parties and, to this end, it is necessary to protect the weakest party in this relationship: the employee (CASSAR, 2015).

This protection of the worker advocated by Labor Law is subjectively configured as a form of protection for the dignity of the human person. Labor law is also a competent instrument that guarantees and protects the worker - the weakest, most hyposufficient party in employment relationships.

According to Cassar (2015, p.7):

> Labor law is a legal system permeated by instruments, values, rules and principles aimed at subordinate and similar workers, employers, affiliated companies, service takers, for the protection of the minimum employment contract, obligations arising from employment relationships, measures aimed at protecting the working society, always guided by constitutional principles, especially the dignity of the human person.

Thus, it is clear that the principle of human dignity is the basis or benchmark for the construction of legal systems and legislation regulating conduct governed by labor law. This law is dynamic as society advances in its paradigm shifts as a result of the transformations induced by the progress of science and technology. Thus, for example, the Constitutional Amendment Bill (PEC) 72/2013 signals achievements for the working class, specifically domestic workers, promoting greater justice and recognition of the right to dignity for workers.

According to Cordeiro (2012, p.70), Article 427 of the Treaty of Versailles of 1919, which gave rise to labor law, is guided in its construction by some elements that make up the principle of human dignity, as can be seen below:

1 - The guiding principle set out above that work should not be considered a commodity or an article of commerce;

2 - The right to associate in order to achieve any objective not contrary to the law, for both employers and employees;

3 - The payment to workers of a wage that guarantees them an adequate standard of living in relation to their time and country;

4 - The adoption of an eight-hour working day or a forty-eight-hour week;

5 - The adoption of a 24-hour rest week, whenever possible on Sundays;

6 - The suppression of child labor and the obligation to impose the necessary limitations on the work of minors of both sexes to enable them to continue their

education and ensure their physical development.
7 - The principle of equal pay, without distinction of sex, for work of equal value.
8 - The laws enacted in each country regarding working conditions shall ensure equitable economic treatment for all workers legally residing in the country;
9 - Each state shall organize an inspection service, including women, to ensure the application of laws and regulations for the protection of workers.

In this way, it becomes clear that the Principle of Human Dignity has permeated the foundations of Labor Law since before its origin. Thus, as the aforementioned author states: "in international and constitutional texts, the dignity of the human person has become a legal command indissolubly linked to the concept of human rights, as their source and justification and as a guiding principle for state action" (CORDEIRO, 2012). All of this is configured as the intention to protect workers.

The principle of worker protection is evident in Brazil's permanent state intervention in relations between employer and employee, substantially restricting the parties' autonomy of will. Thus, the state legislates and imposes minimum rules that must be followed by social agents. These will form the basic structure of every employment contract.

It is because of this principle that labor law has seen the need to protect employees, safeguarding their right to decent work, respecting the human condition and the minimum required to sustain life.

However, it can be said that the Principle of the Dignity of the Human Person within Labor Law acts as a guiding instrument for the smooth running of labor relations, placing limits on the claims stipulated in employment contracts, considered fair and dignified, so that the worker can achieve an improvement in his socio-economic condition[1] .

This improvement has not reached domestic workers, due to the lack of support in the specific legislation of labor law - the Consolidation of Labor Laws (CLT), where domestic workers are excluded from this protection in accordance with art. 7, point "a": "The precepts contained in this Consolidation, unless expressly stated otherwise in each case, do not apply to: a) domestic workers, who are generally considered to be those who provide services of a non-economic nature to a person or

1 - Available at:http://docplaYer.com.br/15068860-Unifavip-devrY-centro-universit.. Accessed on: Aug. 28, 2016.

family, in their residential environment[2] .

This is a legal contradiction in terms, because if the law guarantees workers' rights, there is no way that domestic workers can be excluded from its protection by having to resort to a special law, which does not grant them equality with other workers. In this way, the dignity and equality of people are usurped, which are fundamental principles that cannot be violated, under penalty of the penalties provided by law for those who do so.

2- http://www.jusbrasil.com.br/topicos/10766113/artigo-7-do-decreto-lei-n-5452-de-01-de-maio-de-1943. Accessed on: Aug. 28, 2016.

3. A BRIEF HISTORY OF OUTSOURCING

Driven by new technologies and new ways of working, modern companies are undergoing profound transformations. Many are expanding, while others are shrinking or merging, and most are transforming as they seek out the partnerships that bring production networks to life. Those that fail to adapt to these transformations run the serious risk of going out of business.

With the phenomenon of globalization and, consequently, the increase in competitiveness between companies, it has become obligatory to rethink working relationships, because the balance of companies and, concomitantly, their own production capacity and competitiveness in the market, which increasingly demands excellence in the provision of services and quality in their products, depend on these relationships.

It was in this context that outsourcing emerged as a proposal to solve the problems inherent in the efficiency of companies and their need to become increasingly competitive in the globalized market.

Thus, according to Delgado (2012, p. 419):

> Outsourcing, for this reason, has been used on a large scale by companies in all branches of production, as a management practice that allows companies to delegate activities and reduce costs by transferring part of the company's management process in various sectors (production, food, cleaning) to employees of other companies who are only hired to provide a specific service. It is therefore possible to simply define outsourcing as *"the process by which a company stops performing one or more activities carried out by directly hired workers and transfers them to another company."*

Corroborating the words of the aforementioned author, it can be said that outsourcing is, in fact, of immeasurable value to contemporary companies, which are forced to seek excellence and competitiveness in today's globalized market scenario.

For Pastore and Pastore (2015):

> The outsourcing process itself has undergone a major metamorphosis. It needs to be constantly updated. The first phase, so to speak, took place in the 1970s, when the outsourcing process involved only the peripheral activities of companies and was basically oriented towards cost reduction, such as security, cleaning, food and others.
>
> In the second phase, which took place in the mid-1980s, companies began to outsource activities close to their *core business,* and improving the quality of services was just as important as reducing costs. The relationship between partners became strategically important. It was during this phase that services such as the creation of new products, research and development, the purchase of tailor-made systems and others began to be outsourced, even to companies located abroad.

As is clear, outsourcing has taken on international proportions, which demonstrates its importance for companies because, despite other interpretations, it has provided many benefits, increasing companies' profit margins and creating jobs.

The third phase, which began in the mid-1990s, was driven by the need to overcome the intense competition between global companies and, above all, between global value chains. In this phase, companies set out to contract out stages of their *core business* and rely on these services in real time. With technical rigor and quality. According to Pastore and Pastore (2015, p. 32):

> Today, the decision to outsource has changed. Today, executives are being asked to adopt a strategic role in order to stimulate innovation and competitive advantage. Thus, by gaining productive efficiency, companies perform their social function better, especially that of generating good quality jobs, protecting workers and paying decent wages and benefits, as outsourcing enthusiasts claim.

The search for increased productivity, new models of work organization and new management techniques has meant that companies are increasingly forced to decentralize their activities so that they can be carried out by other work centers. Outsourcing makes this model viable. These organizational and economic "arrangements", in turn, generate legal effects.

It was in the 1970s that outsourcing began to be implemented in Brazil, and soon after it was consolidated throughout the country, through the adoption of the Toyotist model of division of labor.

Without the existence of specific legislation on outsourcing, but only sparse legislation regulating certain services and cases, companies have created new production strategy techniques *(just in time),* quality programs and the outsourcing of services.

According to Queiros (2010, p.63):

> Outsourcing emerged in the United States of America in the 1950s as an evolving productive alternative. In Brazil, outsourcing began to be implemented and developed by the advent of multinationals, mainly in the 1980s, and was then known, around 1989, as third-party contracting. The aim of "outsourcing" was already to reduce costs, as well as to generate an increase in quality, efficiency, specialization, effectiveness and productivity.

Outsourcing basically consists of hiring third parties for the contracting company's middle activities, i.e. to carry out activities that are not its core business. Thus, the work is carried out for one company, but hired immediately by another.

According to Giosa (2010, p.13), outsourcing is characterized as a modern management technique, since the outsourced company mediates between the service taker and the outsourced workforce.

According to Barros (2010, p. 424):

> Outsourcing "consists of transferring activities that are considered secondary, i.e. support activities, to others, with the company sticking to its core business". The aim of outsourcing is to reduce costs and at the same time improve the quality of the product or service.

A broader concept of outsourcing is provided by Delgado (2009, p.430):

> For labor law, outsourcing is the phenomenon whereby the employment relationship is dissociated from the corresponding labor-justice relationship. This phenomenon inserts the worker into the production process of the service provider without extending to the latter the labor law boundaries, which are preserved by an intervening entity. Outsourcing creates a trilateral relationship when it comes to hiring labor in the capitalist market: the worker, who provides services and carries out his material and intellectual activities for the company that takes over the services; the outsourcing company, which hires this worker and signs the relevant labor law contracts with him; and the company that takes over the services, which receives the services but does not assume the classic position of employer of the worker involved.

The phenomenon of outsourcing is advancing on all continents with the main objective of the borrowing company dedicating itself to its core business, seeking to produce good products at low prices. It involves the hiring of services rather than a specific, subordinate or temporary worker, presenting itself as a trend towards the return of labor law relations to civil law (DELGADO, 2009).

In this way, the company contracting the services has more time to control and manage its own business, which brings benefits and improvements for the contracting company. In fact, the decentralization of the company's activities, which are transferred to outsourced services, allows the company to focus more on its core business.

Outsourcing has been a controversial issue not only in legal circles, but also among workers, workers' associations, cooperatives and unions. It is therefore, without a shadow of a doubt, a delicate subject that needs to be analyzed in the light of Labor Law and with a lot of common sense, so that there are no setbacks in the labor rights achieved, nor does it cause financial losses for the worker, who is already very exploited in Brazil.

4. OUTSOURCING

There is no escaping this reality, because outsourcing is part of our daily lives, as has already been said, and is a reality in labor relations, all due to the fluctuations in the economy, financial speculation, increased competitiveness, the search for profit alone and the malleability of laws.

Although there is no legislation that defines outsourcing, it is up to the doctrine to conceptualize it. However, some concepts can be found in administrative and legal doctrines. Moraes (2003, p.99) presents some concepts about outsourcing. According to Livio Giosa (2003, p.64), outsourcing is:

> [...] a management process whereby certain activities are passed on to third parties, with whom a partnership relationship is established, leaving the company to concentrate only on tasks essentially linked to the business in which it operates.

For Ciro Pereira da Silva (2003, p.65), outsourcing can be defined as:

> [...] the transfer of activities to specialized suppliers, with their own modern technology, who have this outsourced activity as their core business, freeing the borrower to concentrate its management efforts on its core business, preserving and evolving in quality and productivity, reducing costs and gaining competitiveness.

Legal experts see outsourcing from a different angle. While administrators see outsourcing as an important tool for corporate profit, the legal community analyzes the institute based on the dynamics of the relationships between the outsourcing and outsourced legal entities (MORAES, 2003, p. 66).

According to Catharino (2005, p.107): "there is great polemic about the activities that can or cannot be outsourced, most of which conceive the outsourcing process only when related to middle or complementary activities".
According to Barros (2003, p.67):

> Outsourcing is a phenomenon that consists of transferring activities that are considered secondary, or support activities, more properly called middle activities, to others, with the company dedicating itself to its main activity, i.e. its core business.

According to Martins (2003, p.67): "the possibility of hiring third parties to carry out the company's middle activities, that is, those activities that do not constitute its main object, its essential activity".

According to the aforementioned author, outsourcing means assigning an activity that is not related to the main objective of the company taking on the services to another company, so that it hires its own employees, maintaining an employment relationship with them. The outsourced company is an intermediary in the relationship, which becomes trilateral, according to Delgado (2002, p.417):

> This phenomenon inserts the worker into the production process of the service provider without extending to the latter the just labor laws, which remain fixed with an intervening entity. Outsourcing creates a trilateral relationship when it comes to hiring labor in the capitalist market: the worker, a service provider, who carries out his material and intellectual activities for the company that takes over the services; the outsourcing company, which hires this worker and signs the relevant labor law contracts with him; and the company that takes over the services, which receives the services but does not assume the classic position of employer of the worker involved.

Generally speaking, the use of outsourcing techniques includes de-verticalization, which means passing on functions to a specialized supplier who manufactures the components requested by the service taker; the provision of services is the most common form of outsourcing and is characterized when a third party carries out the middle activity of the service taker, performing it on the latter's premises or at a predetermined location; the purchase of services, which occurs when a company with saturated capacity needs to increase its activities and goes in search of partners to complement its production capacity; the appointment of representatives, which occurs when a company hires another company or companies to represent it in general sales.

According to Cherchglia (2002, p. 80):

> It also includes concessions, which occur when a company acts on behalf of another, which conditions the use of its brand and the marketing of its products; permissions, typically used in the outsourcing of public services, occur when the operation of a public service is passed on to a permissionaire so that it can exclusively operate the service, and finally the allocation of labor, which is the purchase or rental of working hours, and can be developed as temporary or unionized work.

According to Mariangela Leal Cherchglia (2002, p.81): "other forms of application of the technique, such as disintegration, faction, corporatization, integrated decentralization, are specific to a particular branch of the economy or are still incipient."

Therefore, according to Americo (2004, p.66):

> The company that takes on the services can focus solely on the production of the main object, increasing productivity and quality, as well as reducing production costs. That said, while in the traditional model the employee provides services directly to the employer, with whom he has an employment relationship (art. 2, *caput,* CLT), in outsourcing the relationship is trilateral,

> where the employee provides services to the borrower, although he is not its actual employee. The employment relationship is established with another party, the intermediary, intervening or supplier company.

4.1 PRINCIPLES OF LABOR LAW AND OUTSOURCING

Outsourcing must comply with the principles of Labor Law, and in this regard, art. 4 of the Law of Introduction to the Civil Code states that: "when the law is silent, the judge shall decide the case according to analogy, custom and the general principles of law".

Thus, it is understood in this article that it is up to judges to develop the law when there is a gap in the legislation, with the aim of reaching the most favorable decision in the specific case. Therefore, in the absence of legislation to deal with the issue in question, a solution must be sought through the systematic interpretation of our legal system, mainly in the principles contained in the Federal Constitution of 1988 and the CTL.

Principles are a legal structure whose main objective is to enable the application of rules in specific cases. They are of great importance in the legal system, as they guide the law and have informative, interpretative and normative characteristics in the law.

In Labor Law, Article 8 of the CLT gives the principles an essential function, stating that they should be applied in the event of a legal or contractual omission, *in verbis:*

> Art. 8 - The administrative authorities and the Labor Court, in the absence of legal or contractual provisions, shall decide, as the case may be, by case law, analogy, equity and other general principles and rules of law, especially labor law, and also in accordance with custom and comparative law, but always in such a way that no class or private interest prevails over the public interest.
> Sole paragraph. Common law shall be a subsidiary source of labor law insofar as it is not incompatible with the fundamental principles of the latter.
> Therefore, labor law, as an autonomous law, has its own principles that constitute specific foundations of the labor legal system, not to be confused with other branches of law (ARTICLE 8 of the CLT).

In view of the above, it is safe to say that the principles that govern labor law are essential as guidelines for all employment relationships. With this in mind, Rodriguez (2002, p.50) points out:

> The importance of the principles of this branch of the law is paramount, emphasizing that they constitute the foundation of the labor legal system and,

> consequently, there can be no contradiction between them and the legal precepts. Furthermore, it is true to say that these principles are above positive law, in that they serve as an inspirational element, but they cannot become independent of the system, since they influence each other.

Thus, the basic principles of Labor Law that are pertinent to this topic under discussion are:

1 - The principle of protection - which is broken down into three other principles aimed at guaranteeing better conditions for workers, as well as applying the most favorable rules, with the aim of correcting inequalities in the face of the employee's position of hyposufficiency.

The purpose of the above-mentioned principle is to balance the relationship between the employer and the workforce, which is almost always unequal. Inequality between human beings is a phenomenon that has existed since its inception, when the strongest has always maintained a privileged position of superiority in any favorable situation, and even in subjecting the other to forced labor.

However, on the scope of this principle, the following teaching is extracted, according to Americo (2004, p.39):

> [...] this principle does not give the right to do anything in the name of worker protection, much less to substitute itself for the creator of the rules. It has a limited field of application and, by staying within it, it does not conspire against safety, but ensures the effective and appropriate application of the rule.

2 - The principle of "In dubio pro operario" - aims to protect the weakest party in the employment relationship: the worker. This principle states that when there is doubt as to the interpretation of the rule, the one that is best for the worker should be applied. Of course, this principle must be applied rationally, seeking to respect the will of the legislator.

The nature of this principle is considered to be hermeneutic, because if there is a provision in a law or a contract that leaves room for interpretation in a dubious sense, the rule is that the interpretation that brings the most benefit to the worker will be adopted.

3 - The principle of "applying the most favorable rule" - will be used whenever there is a plurality of rules, and once again the one that most favors the worker must be chosen.

It is known that there are various rules that regulate labor relations, such as: normative sentences, collective agreements, conventions, internal company regulations, etc. It is important to point out that when applying this principle there will be no hierarchy of rules, but rather the application of the one that is best for the worker.

4 - The principle of the most beneficial condition - this principle is closely linked to the principle of the most favorable rule. In this case, the aim is to maintain the rights and privileges achieved by the worker during the employment contract.

Art. 10 of the CLT states: "Any change in the company's legal structure shall not affect the rights acquired by its employees".

Along the same lines, art. 468 of the CLT states:

> Individual employment contracts may only be altered by mutual consent, and even then provided that the employee is not directly or indirectly harmed, failing which the clause infringing this guarantee will be null and void.

In this understanding, the application of this principle can be found in Sumula 51 of the TST, *in verbis:*

> I- Regulatory clauses that revoke or alter previously granted benefits will only affect workers hired after the revocation or alteration of the regulation.
> II - If two company regulations coexist, the employee's opting in to one of them has the legal effect of waiving the rules of the other system (ex-OJ No. 163 of SBDI-1 - inserted on 26.03.1999) (SUMULA 51 TST).

It is easy to understand from this reading of the above-mentioned Summula that no changes can be made to the employment contract that would harm the worker. If there is any change that leads to a reduction in benefits, it will only affect workers who are hired later.

In this way, the benefits and guarantees provided for in the employment contract are guaranteed to the worker, and the employer is forbidden to revoke or refrain from these guarantees unilaterally and to his detriment.

5 - The principle of the primacy of reality - also known as primacy over form, this principle states that in the event of a dissonance between factual reality and existing documents or contracts, the former will prevail, based on the real truth, since the reality of the facts is not susceptible to tampering by human will and documents can inaccurately express the will of the parties, as well as being vitiated by formative defects that jeopardize their validity.

According to Johnston (2002, p.122): "the objective relationship evidenced by the facts defines the true legal relationship stipulated by the contracting parties, even if in a simulated guise, not corresponding to reality"

The principle of the primacy of reality arises from the rule in Article 9 of the

CLT: "Acts carried out with the aim of distorting, preventing or defrauding the application of the precepts contained in this Consolidation shall be null and void".

In this way, it is understood, according to Sumula 331 of the TST, that based on this principle, in Labor Law the "reality contract" will prevail, i.e. regardless of any contract or documents that give the appearance of regularity, if the fact is disputed, reality will prevail. The CLT provides for the possibility of hiring employees even tacitly, i.e. independently of a contract.

Still on the subject of principles, the prevalence of the autonomy of will in contracts in general, according to Johnston (2002, p.123):

> It does not apply to employment contracts because of the principle of non-renounceability of labor rights, which prevents employees from waiving rights arising from the employment relationship that have been granted to them by the State. Therefore, as a rule, the employee's silence or agreement to the suppression of any of his rights arising from the employment relationship will have no effect, as the State does not grant him the power to waive them.

As the rule is non-renounceability, the exception only occurs when the legal norm expressly grants the employee the right to carry out the act.

Americo (2004, p.66) conceptualizes this principle as being: "the legal impossibility of voluntarily depriving oneself of one or more advantages granted by the

Labor Law for their own benefit". And he adds that "renunciation is equivalent to a voluntary act by which a person withdraws from a right recognized in their favour and abandons it" (AMERICO, 2004, p. 67).

6 - The principle of good faith - Sumula 331 of the TST: good faith is not a rule, but a fundamental legal principle. It is legitimate conduct without harming third parties, or loyalty, in the sense of honesty, which is what prevails in Labor Law, and is presented from two angles: subjective, which is esteem, and legal, which is outward conduct. It must exist between both parties and represents the ethical value of work.

One of the foundations of the Federal Constitution (1988) is the basic principle of the entire legal system: the dignity of the human person. Art.1 The Federative Republic of Brazil, formed by the indissoluble union of States and Municipalities and the Federal District, is a Democratic State governed by the rule of law and has as its foundations: [...] III - the dignity of the human person.

Morais (2007, p.16) teaches about the importance of this principle:

> [...] it gives unity to fundamental rights and guarantees, being inherent to human personalities. this foundation removes the idea of the predominance of transpersonalist conceptions of state and nation, to the detriment of

individual freedom. the dignity of the human person is a spiritual and moral value inherent to the person, which manifests itself uniquely in the conscious and responsible self-determination of one's own life and which brings with it the claim to respect from other people, constituting an invulnerable minimum that every legal statute must guarantee, so that only exceptionally can limitations be made to the exercise of fundamental rights, but always without belittling the necessary esteem that all people deserve as human beings.

It is also known as the principle of human value, which consists of the humanization of work, in considering the worker as a human being and not as a commodity or element of production.

4.1.1 Tendered outsourcing

Currently, in Brazil, the main regulator of tendered outsourcing is the Sumula 331, of the TST, which clarifies the peculiarities of the issue brought up: Sumula No. 331 of the TST:

> Service Contract - Legality
>
> I - The hiring of workers by an intermediary company is illegal, and the relationship is formed directly with the service provider, except in the case of temporary work (Law No. 6.019, of January 3, 1974).
> II - The irregular hiring of a worker through an intermediary company does not create an employment relationship with direct, indirect or foundational public administration bodies (art. 37, II, CF/1988).
> III - The hiring of security services (Law No. 7.102, of 20-06-1983), maintenance and cleaning services, as well as specialized services linked to the borrower's core business, does not form an employment relationship with the borrower, as long as there is no personal relationship and no direct subordination.
> IV - The employer's failure to comply with its labor obligations implies that the borrower of the services is liable for those obligations, including direct administration bodies, municipalities, public foundations, public companies and mixed-capital companies, provided that they have participated in the procedural relationship and are also included in the judicial enforcement order (art. 71 of Law No. 8.666, of 06.21.1993).

At this point, it can be divided into four items to visualize the situations of licit outsourcing:

I- Temporary Work (Sumula 331, I, TST);

II- Surveillance Services (Sumula 331, III, TST);

III- Maintenance and cleaning services (Sumula 331, I, TST);

IV- Specialized services linked to the borrower's core business (Sumula 331, I, TST).

The first item refers to business situations that authorize the hiring of temporary work. These situations are expressly contained in Law No. 6.019/74 and refer to the need arising from an extraordinary increase in the company's services or the temporary need to replace regular or permanent staff at the borrowing company, such as, for example, replacement during holidays or maternity leave.

The second item is governed by Law No. 7.102/83 and deals with surveillance services. Sumula 331, TST has broadened the legal type, since Sumula 256 of the same Court referred exclusively to the cases provided for in the aforementioned law, and today, the new Sumula broadly mentions surveillance activities. Any segment of the labor market that hires surveillance services from a specialized company can use the legal instrument of outsourcing.

It is worth noting that shortly after Sumula 331 was issued, with a broad interpretation, the legislator made changes to Law No. 7.102/83, through Law No. 8.863/94.

The third item corresponds to maintenance and cleaning activities.

These activities were among the first to be outsourced to the private sector in Brazil. Maintenance and cleaning can be of property or monuments, such as cleaning, window cleaning, janitorial services, gardening, among others.

The fourth and final item refers to specialized services linked to the borrower's middle activities. These middle activities are not expressly discriminated against, but they are activities that are not at the core of the service provider's activity, i.e. they are different from the core activities.

In the last three groups mentioned above, outsourcing will only remain lawful if there is no personal and direct legal subordination between the outsourced worker and the service taker (Sumula 331, III, *in fine*, TST).

The debate about what is a core activity and what is an end activity has been going on for a long time. Garcia (2008, p. 67) clarifies: "middle activity is that of mere support, which does not integrate the core, that is, the essence, of the business activities of the borrower, being the end activity, therefore, that which composes it".

Delgado (1999, p.365) explains:

> End-activities can be conceptualized as the business and labor functions and tasks that fit into the core of the business dynamics of the service provider, making up the essence of this dynamics and even contributing to the definition of its positioning and classification in the business and economic context. They are therefore core activities that define the essence of the service provider's business dynamics. On the other hand, middle activities are those business and labor functions and tasks that do not fit into the core of the service provider's business dynamics, nor do they make up the essence of those dynamics or contribute to defining its position in the broader business and economic context. They are therefore peripheral activities to

the essence of the service provider's business dynamics.

The majority of outsourcing in Brazil can be easily transformed from licit to illicit, since in almost all cases the worker is directly personal and subordinate to the service provider.

According to Sussekind (2001, p.39):

> If the worker registered as an employee of the contracted firm provides services to the contractor under the latter's power of command, the employment relationship with the latter is established, based on the principle of the primacy of reality, which is widely accepted in Labor Law (...).

As a result, the principle of the primacy of reality is applicable in labor law, based on the actual truth of the facts, without taking into account the name or form given to the legal transaction.

Therefore, it is understood that the national doctrine is unanimous on the idea that outsourcing is the possibility of hiring a third party to carry out activities that are not the core business of the borrowing company.

4.1.2 Illegal outsourcing and its consequences in the legal world

It is common knowledge that outsourcing is not prohibited in our legal system, but it is forbidden under the terms of Sumula 331, I, of the Superior Labor Court. From the above-mentioned Summula, it can be concluded that: firstly, it is illegal to outsource services considered to be the "core business" of the company taking over the services, and the employment relationship is formed directly with the latter, except in the case of temporary work and, secondly; even if the outsourcing is of services considered to be "core business", if there is personal and subordinate relationship with the company taking over the services, the employment relationship is formed directly with the company taking over the services.

In line with this reasoning, we have the following case law:

> ORDINARY APPEAL. OUTSOURCING. NULLITY OF THE CONTRACT BETWEEN THE EMPLOYEE AND THE COMPANY PROVIDING SERVICES. FORMATION OF THE EMPLOYMENT RELATIONSHIP DIRECTLY WITH THE SERVICE PROVIDER. BANKING INSTITUTION. RIGHTS OF A NORMATIVE NATURE. APPLICABLE. The legal system does not accept subcontracting in the contracting company's core business. Portuguese law follows the line that has built rules seeking to insert the worker into the company, guaranteeing the continuity of the contract and preventing the worker's energy from being the target of unjustified exploitation. These rules are enshrined in international labor law. Once the intermediation of labor has been established, the rule of art. 9 of the

> Consolidation of Labor Laws applies, and the guidelines of Sumula n. 331, I, of the TST apply, forming the relationship directly with the company that takes on the services. Since the contractor belongs to the economic category of credit establishments, the plaintiff is entitled to receive the salaries and other benefits provided for bank employees in collective bargaining agreements. (TRT6ª R.; Proc. 000001794.2011.5.06.0022; Second Panel; Rel.ª Desª Eneida Melo Correia de Araujo; Julg. 05/10/2011; DEJTPE 13/10/2011; Pag. 80)

> LABOR LAW. PROCEDURAL LABOR LAW. UNION FRAMEWORK. ORDINARY APPEAL BY THE DEFENDANTS. Under Brazilian law, an employee's union membership is based on the company's preponderant activity, in accordance with the provisions of articles 577 and 581, paragraph 2, of the CLT, except in the case of a differentiated professional category, pursuant to the concept set out in paragraph 3 of article 511 of the Consolidated Law, which is not the case here. Since the first defendant is a multiple bank and is recognized as the plaintiff's real employer, the plaintiff must be included in the banking category, and is entitled to payment of the amounts arising from the collective bargaining agreements signed, on the one hand, by the National Federation of Banks - FENABAN - and other employers' unions and, on the other, by the National Confederation of Workers in Financial Institutions - CNTIF - and their respective professional unions, because this representativeness of the collective entities involved is evident. AGREE the members of the Third Panel of the Regional Labor Court of the 6ª Region, unanimously, to dismiss the ordinary appeal. Recife, September 21, 2011. (TRT6ª R.; Proc. 0000685-41.2010.5.06.0009; Third Panel; Rel.ª Desª Virginia Malta Canavarro; Julg. 21/09/2011; DEJTPE 04/10/2011).

However, the legal exceptions are restricted to the hypotheses provided for by Law No. 6.019/74 (Temporary Work) and Law No. 7.102/83 (Surveillance, Cleaning and Conservation).

Even so, we can see from these laws that such outsourcing is only allowed to meet the company's temporary need to replace its regular and permanent staff or for the extraordinary increase in services, and for surveillance, cleaning and maintenance services, as long as there is no presence of direct subordination and personality.

It can be seen that the sole paragraph of art. 170 of the Federal Constitution, although it authorizes the free exercise of any economic activity, consists of a principle-based rule and is by no means intended to regulate the activity of outsourcing in the context of labor relations. To interpret it differently would be to authorize the indiscriminate practice of outsourcing and, consequently, the devaluation of human labor, in clear offense to a series of historically conquered labor norms and principles.

However, faced with the need to protect the labor market from this inevitable and increasingly growing phenomenon in labor relations in our country and around the world, the Superior Labor Court issued Sumula 331. Through item III of Sumula 331, the TST added to our legal system the possibility of outsourcing middle activities, i.e. those that are not related to the main object of the company's economic activity.

And the above-mentioned Summula, to this day, remains the only legal institute that regulates the outsourcing of other activities in our legal system, other than those dealt with in Laws 6.019/74 and 7.102/83.

However, the Superior Labor Court has made it clear that, even in the case of "middle-management activities", outsourcing will be considered illegal when the requirements of personal and subordinate employment are present, and the employment relationship is formed directly with the company that takes on the services.

According to Chahad and Cacciamali (2003, p.53), outsourcing:

> It is the subcontracting of companies that provide workers so that the organization can carry out its middle or peripheral activities, thus freeing it to concentrate its productive efforts on its core business.

The violation of the legal precepts raised in the text violates labor rights and is an affront to the dignity of the worker, since human work in illicit outsourcing is transformed into a simple commodity, which goes against the foundations of the Federative Republic of Brazil, being the dignity of the human person and the social values of work, contained in Article 1, items III and IV of the Federal Constitution of 1988.

Article 581, paragraph 2 of the CLT states that: "the end activity is understood to be that which characterizes the unity of the product, operation or final objective, to the achievement of which all other activities converge exclusively in a functionally connected regime". However, the distinction between middle and end activities is complicated precisely because there is no detailed definition of the concept of each.

Therefore, outsourcing must be aimed at performing specialized services, i.e. services that are not indispensable or permanent within the scope of the productive activity of the service taker, but rather, consistent with an exceptional situation and of a fixed duration.

However, the following must be noted: if unlawful outsourcing is characterized, the employment relationship with the service provider must be established. Therefore, the above rule can only be applied if the service provider is private, in which case, if the service provider is the State, i.e. the Direct or Indirect Public Administration, the rule does not apply.

In view of this, the government is privileged, since it is not allowed to establish an employment relationship with the outsourced worker without a public tender, even if it is illegal outsourcing, which would violate Sumula 331, II, TST, which states: "The irregular hiring of a worker, through an intermediary company, does not generate an employment relationship with public administration bodies, direct, indirect or foundational".

Questions about this issue are growing all the time. In the case of subcontracting, where the contracting company does not pay the worker's labor rights, according to Sumula 331, TST, the service taker has subsidiary liability, regardless of whether it is private or public. This is what item IV of the Summula says:

> The employer's failure to comply with its labor obligations implies that the service provider will be held liable for those obligations, including the bodies of the direct administration, municipalities, public foundations, public companies and mixed-capital companies, provided that they have participated in the procedural relationship and are also included in the judicial enforcement order.

Thus, when workers default on their labor obligations, they file a labor claim with the Labor Courts and the companies that provide the services, for the most part, do not have the assets to guarantee payment of these obligations. The service providers, therefore, generally incur *"in elegendo" or "in vigilando"* guilt (usually concurrently) and are therefore subsidiarily liable for labor obligations (BARROS, 2007).

Therefore, the right thing to do would be for the law to make the service provider jointly and severally liable for the outsourcer's labor debts, as this would be a way of giving the outsourcer greater security.

According to Barros (2007, p.447):

> The main employer, except for the expiry of the period mentioned above with regard to social security, and during the year following the end of its contract, will be jointly and severally liable for the wage obligations contracted by subcontractors with their workers and for those relating to social security during the period of validity of the contract, limited to what would have been the case if it had hired permanent staff in the same category or workplaces.

If the outsourcing is illegal, there are two possibilities: if it's a private company, you can claim recognition of the employment relationship. In the case of a public company, i.e. the government, you can claim equal pay for the entire period worked, including all the rights of the category.

4.1.3 Outsourcing and the Theory of Structural Subordination

Although apparently simple, the issue is truly complex. This type of employment relationship, in particular, where there are countless and creative business maneuvers to distort the employment relationship, has given rise to the Theory of Structural Subordination, emplaced by the illustrious doctrinaire and jurist Mauricio Godinho Delgado (2008), according to which the flexibility and liberality of the production chain dispense with the direct order of the employer, who now only orders production as a whole, but even so, does not rule out the formation of a direct link with the borrowing company.

It is also worth transcribing the judgment below, which clearly demonstrates the application of this theory to the specific case:

> OUTSOURCING AND STRUCTURAL SUBORDINATION. While working as a telephone cable installer/splicer, the plaintiff performed a function that was perfectly and essentially part of the business activities of the telephone company (TELEMAR). And once he was part of this essential context of the productive activity of the post-industrial and flexible company, there was no longer any need for direct orders from the employer, who only ordered production. In this post-big-industry environment, it is up to the worker to "collaborate". The new organization of work, through the system of flexible accumulation, imbues a kind of competitive cooperation between workers that does away with the classic system of hierarchy. To a certain extent, competition has been displaced from the field of capital and introduced into the sphere of work, since the team of workers itself is in charge of charging each other to increase the group's productivity; there is a kind of horizontal subrogation of the employer's command. The traditional legal subordinate system was designed for the reality of Fordist and Taylorist production, which was highly hierarchical and segmented. There, the binomial order-subordination prevailed. In the ohnist system, with flexible management, the collaboration-dependence binomial prevails, which is more in line with a structuralist conception of subordinations. In this vein, it is irrelevant to discuss the illegality or otherwise of outsourcing, as well as the provisions of art. 94, II of Law 9.472/97, because in the factual context in which this case is examined, the evidence shows that the plaintiff-worker is subordinated to the telecommunications enterprise, an enterprise whose final beneficiary of the surplus human labor is the telephone company. It is worth remembering that in the happy and contemporary conceptualization of the CLT - article 2, caput - the typical employer is the company and not a specific entity endowed with legal personality. The employment relationship arises from the economic reality of the company and the enterprise, but is perfected as a result of the final entity benefiting from the business activities. (TRT 3ª R First Class 00059- 2007-011-03-00-0 RO Ordinary Appeal Judge Jose Eduardo de Resende Chaves Junior DJMG 03/08/2007 P.4).

Therefore, this new model must be recognized, because structural subordination will be the only or last way for workers to obtain decent payment for their work in this labor dynamic as outsourced workers. The efforts of jurisprudence and society have the sole purpose of curbing such illegal practices.

5. EQUAL PAY

Illicit outsourcing has become an increasingly widespread practice and since a large part of these precarious labor contracts are made with the state, which is the service taker, a legal solution to this situation was sought.

The measures that have been taken the most today are to ensure that salaries are equal, even if the employment relationship with the state is not recognized, in compliance with the precepts of article 37, II of the Federal Constitution, which states:

> Admission to public office or employment depends on prior approval in a public examination of tests or tests and titles, according to the nature and complexity of the office or employment, as provided by law, with the exception of appointments to commissioned positions declared by law to be freely appointable and exonerable.

The fact that recognition of a direct relationship with the government is forbidden does not cancel out the blatant irregularity of illegal outsourcing and does not establish an advantage in the exploitation of human labor in favor of public entities.

Cavalcante Junior (1996, p. 173) explains:

> One of the effects of outsourcing in the public administration: "Outsourcing in the public sector can cause, in relation to the workers involved in it, patrimonial damages due to the non-receipt of labor rights".
> The path to be followed is also in our Constitution, when Article 5, caput, *ab* initio and item I, guarantees the observance of isonomy, which, in one way or another, tries to mitigate the effects left by this practice. Article 7, XXXII of the Constitution also contains the fundamental precept that it is forbidden to distinguish between manual, technical and intellectual work or between the respective professionals.

According to Barros (2007, p. 450):

> The isonomy alluded to in article 461 of the Consolidated Law applies exceptionally when different employers are involved, i.e. in the case of temporary workers, whose pay must be the same as that earned by an employee with the same job at the borrower or client company, in accordance with the command contained in Law No. 6.019 of 1974. The same reasoning applies, by virtue of Article 5, *caput, of* the Federal Constitution of 1988, to outsourcing, i.e. to employees hired by service providers to provide services to other companies, otherwise there would be a violation of the constitutional principle of equality.

Delgado (2002, p.98) points out how this isonomy would be applied when he says:

> This isonomy would be ensured by guaranteeing the unlawfully outsourced

> worker all the legal and normative labor benefits applicable to the direct state employee, performing the same function in the state entity taking over the services. Or all the legal and normative labor benefits appropriate to the specific function performed by the outsourced worker at the state entity benefiting from the work.

Therefore, according to the aforementioned author, this worker must be guaranteed all the legal and normative labor benefits applicable to direct state employees, i.e. all the wages (13th salary, working hours, night shift bonus, normative wage advantages, etc.). All sums must be paid, but there must be no rectification of the employer's employment record card (CTPS), as this is expressly forbidden by the Constitution.

In practice, the outsourcing company would initially be liable for the sums arising from pay isonomy and communication. In the event of non-payment, according to Sumula 331 of the TST: "the state entity (service taker) would be subsidiarily liable".

Currently, most case law confirms the right to equivalence of wages and rights in unlawful outsourcing. As we can understand from the decision of the Superior Labor Court, which in short states:

> REVIEW APPEAL. Equal pay. Outsourcing. Differences. The current jurisprudence of the SDI-1 of this Court has already decided that it is possible to grant equal pay to the employees of the service taker and the outsourced company, provided that the outsourced company provides services, in its core activity, on equal terms with the employees of the service taker. (E-ED-RR-655028/2000.1, rapporteur: Minister Rosa Maria Weber Candiota da Rosa, DJ 25-05-2007.) Appeal known and upheld". (TST. RR - 854/2005004-21-00. Ac. 3ª Turma. Rapporteur Minister Carlos Alberto Reis de Paula. Publication: DJ - 08-02-2008).

Interesting to bring up a decision of the Individual Disputes Section
- SDI - I, of the Superior Labor Court:

> OUTSOURCING. EQUAL PAY. IDENTITY OF FUNCTIONS BETWEEN THE EMPLOYEES OF THE LABOR SUPPLIER AND THOSE HIRED DIRECTLY BY THE SERVICE TAKER. ARTICLE 12, ALINEA A, OF LAW NO. 6.019/74. ANALOGICAL APPLICATION 1. In the absence of specific legal provision, using analogy and the general principles of law, as well as taking into account the social purposes of the rule applied and the requirements of the common good (LICC, arts. 4 and 5), the precept contained in Article 12(a) of Law No. 6.019/74 is applied to recognize that outsourced employees are treated equally to those hired by the service provider, as long as there is equality of functions. 2. The ordinary legislator made use of this provision in order to curb any discriminatory treatment arising from possible differences in conduct and salaries in the workplace between temporary employees and those in the same category as those employed by the company that takes over the services. Now, if the possibility of discriminatory treatment was seen

> in short-term temporary outsourcing, this circumstance will be much more serious, constant and profound in permanent outsourcing, in which, not infrequently, the service provider's employees are subjected for a prolonged period to conditions of obvious wage inequality in relation to employees of the same category as those of the borrowing company, despite performing identical functions. (3) Motion for a clarification of the case law is known, and is granted, recognizing the right of the Claimants, outsourced workers, to equal pay with the employees of the service provider who perform the same functions, and reinstating the sentence. (TST-E- RR-654.203/00.9, DJ - 11/11/2005, Joao Oreste Dalazen).

Therefore, there is no doubt that if illegal outsourcing takes place and the service provider is a state entity, equal pay must be established so that this type of contracting does not become commonplace.

6. BILL NO. 4.330/2004

Bill No. 4.330/2004 aims to guarantee the protection of all workers involved in outsourcing processes. This bill is currently before the Chamber of Deputies and is being examined by the Constitution and Justice Committee, generating a lot of discussion and controversy and awaiting a final decision.

This project defines the joint responsibility of the contracting and contracted companies with regard to the rights of the contractor's employees, namely: regular payment of monthly remuneration, bonuses, payment of INSS and FGTS contributions, 13th salary, paid rest, holidays and their respective bonuses, among other obligations.

According to Pastore and Pastore (2015, p. 87):

> The proposed regulations will make a decisive contribution to putting an end to the irresponsibility of many service providers who blatantly disregard the rights of their employees. In addition, the bill establishes requirements for contractors to provide a capital guarantee (or insurance). This alone will keep a number of disreputable companies away from outsourcing. In the same vein, the proposal imposes the same treatment for employees of the contractor and the outsourcer as regards the use of cafeterias, outpatient clinics and transportation facilities.

According to the aforementioned authors, guaranteeing these protections is much more important than discussing the need for them.

outsourcing in end-activities or middle-activities, as does the current Sumula No. 331 of the Superior Labor Court, which states:

> **SERVICE CONTRACT. LEGALITY (new wording for item IV and items V and VI inserted) - Res. 174/2011, DEJT disseminated on 27, 30 and 31.05.2011**
>
> I - The hiring of workers by an intermediary company is illegal, and the relationship is formed directly with the service provider, except in the case of temporary work (Law No. 6.019, of January 3, 1974).
>
> II - The irregular hiring of a worker through an intermediary company does not create an employment relationship with direct, indirect or foundational public administration bodies (art. 37, II, CF/1988).
>
> III - The contracting of surveillance services (Law No. 7.102, of 20.06.1983) and maintenance and cleaning services, as well as specialized services linked to the borrower's core business, does not form an employment relationship with the borrower, as long as there is no personal relationship and no direct subordination.
>
> IV - The employer's failure to comply with its labor obligations implies that the service provider is liable for those obligations, provided that it has participated in the procedural relationship and is also included in the judicial

enforcement order.

V - Entities that are part of the direct and indirect Public Administration are liable in the same way as in item IV, if their culpable conduct in complying with the obligations of Law No. 8.666, of 21.06.1993, especially in supervising compliance with the contractual and legal obligations of the service provider as employer, is proven. This responsibility does not arise from mere failure to comply with the labor obligations assumed by the company duly contracted.

VI - The subsidiary liability of the service provider covers all the sums arising from the conviction relating to the period of employment.

Summula 331 of the TST was approved by Administrative Resolution No. 23/93, of December 17, 1993, in accordance with the guidelines of the Special Body of the Superior Labor Court, and was published in the Diario da Justipa da Uniao of December 21, 1993 (p. 28.358), the original wording of item IV was as follows: "the employer's failure to comply with its labor obligations implies the subsidiary liability of the service taker in respect of those obligations, provided that the latter has participated in the procedural relationship and is also included in the judicial enforcement order".

The basis for the entry was Decree-Law no. 200/67, art. 10, § 7, Law no. 5.645/70, art. 3, sole paragraph; Laws no. 6.019/74 and 7.102/83; 1988 Constitution, art. 37, item II (MARTINS, 2012, p. 207).

What's more, Bill 4.330/2004 confirms a number of understandings that have already been consolidated in case law, shows a new concept of outsourced work and regulates the activity of outsourcing companies, making it legal.

In the way it has been constructed, this project has drawn both praise and criticism. However, it cannot be denied that it includes an analysis of the rulings and jurisprudence of the Superior Labor Court, which have guided companies and workers on this issue for a long time.

6.1 IMPORTANT ASPECTS OF BILL NO. 4.330/2004

Bill No. 4.330/2004, according to Pastore and Pastore (2015, p. 89) dces not have a defined structure, due to the small number of articles (only 19), presenting, in its very first article, the limits of application of the law, and affirming the majority understanding of the Superior Labor Court (TST) to apply the Civil Code subsidiarily in the resolution of conflicts arising from the provision of services by third parties, in particular Arts. 421 to 480 (Of Contracts in General) and Arts. 593 to 60 (Of the provision of services). 421 to 480 (Contracts in General) and Arts. 593 to 609 (Service provision):

> Art. 1. This Law regulates service contracts and the employment relationships arising from them, when the service provider is a company that hires employees or subcontracts another company to perform the service.
> Sole paragraph. The provisions of the Civil Code, in particular arts. 421 to 480, and 593 to 609, shall apply subsidiarily to the contract referred to in this Law.

In other words, this Bill No. 4.330/2004, seems to only intend to make outsourcing legal, but leaving the possible issues arising from this outsourcing to be resolved by applying the Civil Code and jurisprudential decisions.

6.1.1 Outsourcing, the Law and the Economy

As a sign of retrogression, for those who don't support the implementation of outsourcing, it is often used as a synonym for precarious labor relations. This ends up influencing the courts, which come to understand that any process of outsourcing is an expedient for making work more precarious. This generalization is exaggerated to say the least.

On this, Robortella (2010, p. 236) states:

> Many consider outsourcing to cause irreparable damage to workers, due to the elimination of legal guarantees and social benefits, as well as the loss of the identity of work. This would even lead to undignified work, breaking the basis of union representation, which would cause, due to the fragmentation of collective union interests, the exposure of outsourced workers to the condition of second-class workers, when they are prevented from enjoying the rights inherent to unionized workers employed by the company that outsources part of its activity.

In fact, the possibility of employees losing some of their labor rights is very worrying, which is why many see outsourcing as a risk that workers will suffer losses. Martins (2012, p. 198) sees outsourcing as a strategy adopted by the company to manage its economic interests well. It is an option that the company makes when it understands that part of its production process can be carried out by an external agent and with greater advantage.

6.1.1.1 Core business and Middle business

In legal circles, there is a lot of doubt as to a definite conceptualization of what is a core activity and what is a middle activity, generating controversy. Thus, according to Melo (2010, p.70):

> Article 581, paragraph 2 of the Consolidated Labor Laws (CLT) states that a core activity is one that characterizes the "unity of the product, operation or final objective, to the achievement of which all other activities converge exclusively in a functionally related regime". However, the distinction between middle and end activities is complicated precisely because there is no detailed definition of the concept of each.

Labor prosecutor Melo (2010, p.71) argues that middle and end activities can be compared to our bodies. Some parts of it are more important than others. For example, the brain is indispensable and cannot be "outsourced", but any individual can survive without a finger or part of a hand. Companies also have activities that are equally indispensable, those that define the company, and other activities that are support activities, which can be outsourced.

In practice, a company's core business is verified by studying its articles of association. If the employee performs any activity that contributes to the production of the company's corporate purpose, he or she is not providing outsourced services, and may have an employment relationship with the service provider recognized, in accordance with Sumula 331 of the TST.

In the case of companies' core activities, outsourcing is limited by Supreme Labor Court Ruling 331. But in practice it does occur. Outsourcing is currently practiced in various sectors, including public administration.

According to Martins (2012, p. 203), the concept of core business is diffuse. The doctrine touches on this element of labor law, but is certainly unable to define precisely what either one is or what the other is. It only interprets on a case-by-case basis and then gives its verdict. Decisions are made by labor judges, who are not always familiar with company management. It is difficult for them to decide precisely how the economic activity of the company should be carried out. However, due to the necessity of their role, they make important decisions. There is no news of countries in which the Labor Court decides in this way.

The issue of the impossibility of defining what a company's core business is because labor law tries to conceptualize a phenomenon that is foreign to it because it is typically economic and extremely dynamic. What is a company's core business today may be its middle business tomorrow, and vice versa. Therefore, the effort to identify what a company's core business is does not prosper in labor law, as this task is simply impossible and unnecessary (MARTINS, 2012).

Outsourcing must be seen as an essentially economic phenomenon, which began with the need to compete, gain productivity and survive. In this way, it carries with it the idea of the company's economic success, provided by the practice of work, especially decent work. As such, there is no way of talking about outsourcing apart from the elements of dignity of those who carry out the work in this model. Social and economic aspects must always be taken into account when talking about labor law. According to Pastore and Pastore (2015, p. 36):

> Outsourcing is an irreversible process. It is an efficient way of combining factors of production in partnership systems. And labor law relates to the economy in this context. True outsourcing is nothing more than coordinated partnership. The modern trend is towards the intensive use of cooperation combined with global competition in order to maintain competitiveness, gain market share and increase investment.

Defending the benefits of outsourcing, the above-mentioned author also states that outsourcing is not synonymous with precariousness, although it is recognized that many service contracts fall outside the protection rules of labor and social security laws. It should be remembered, however, that precarious working conditions are found even among those who are under the legal protection of direct employment, as is the case, for example, with doctors who work as registered employees in three or four hospitals to support their families. The same is true of nurses, high school and college teachers and others.

Referring to the reasons for the spread of outsourcing as a practice adopted by companies, Pires (2011, p. 310) states:

> It is important to note that one of the factors that led to the spread of the outsourcing phenomenon was the brutal competition between companies, which led them to specialize and hire the services of other companies to carry out activities not linked to their core business. The process of outsourcing is associated with focalization, which is the strategy of companies to concentrate their activities on what is the core of the business, facilitating business management, in order to reduce the diversity of ways of organizing production and work. With outsourcing, companies are able to reduce costs and improve performance and quality, since they carry out fewer processes, which is important for facing up to competition.

The regulation of outsourcing by law, even if it is the Bill No. 4.330/2004, approved by the Chamber of Deputies on April 22, 2015, needs to be improved to cover a greater number of worker protections, such as, for example, the access of employees of contractors to facilities at the workplace, such as sanitary facilities, outpatient clinics, restaurants, transportation, etc. It should also provide, as this bill does, for the formation of a fund to guarantee the payment of severance pay at the end of a contract, as well as various other protections.

The approval of Bill No. 4.330/2004 was a defeat for the government, as its political party, the PT (Workers' Party), together with trade union organizations, were calling for its rejection. Its main text was approved on April 8, 2015, after which the Chamber of Deputies considered requests for amendments, known as "highlights".

Bill No. 4.330/2004 has been sent to the Senate, where it will certainly generate controversy. The bill allows companies to outsource even their core activities. Polemics aside, Bill No. 4.330/2004 aims to adapt the practice of outsourcing to the current reality, since, in the world scenario of economic globalization, it is necessary that laws also keep pace with changes.

FINAL CONSIDERATIONS

As we have seen in this article, outsourcing has been confirmed over time as an advantageous way of hiring labor for companies, because it frees them from the heavy social obligations laid down in current legislation.

Outsourcing allows companies to improve quality and reduce costs. However, its legality is in doubt in many cases where companies use this alternative to circumvent the laws in force, getting cheap labor and not paying the social obligations due.

As much as outsourcing is considered beneficial as an administrative resource, bringing results such as the optimization of services and other advantages for the business sector, the more opportunity the company has to circumvent the laws.

There is a great risk that workers' rights will become more precarious when outsourcing. There are those who say that it is advantageous to outsource, even if they are breaking the law, because even if they are caught, the fines are less than the profits made.

According to studies, illicit outsourcing, the main focus of this work, is an increasingly common practice in the Brazilian economic market and despite various discussions between workers, unions, trade unions and government officials, a definitive solution has yet to be found.

The instrument that regulates this issue is Sumula 331 of the TST, which recognizes the legality of outsourcing workers, as long as it does not constitute the company's core business. However, there is controversy over the doctrinal consensus on what outsourcing actually is. This leads to confusion, making it difficult to apply the rule and encouraging the hiring of companies created solely to reduce production costs to the detriment of workers.

The Anamatra magazine (2009) provides alarming data: that year there were more than 9,000 cases before the TST, in which the worker is demanding from the service provider the rights he did not receive from the service provider, and this is extremely serious, violating the principles that guide Labor Law and the Federal Constitution itself.

As such, it is understood that outsourcing should only be used in a licit manner, i.e. when it involves the middle activities of companies, or in situations where the activities are specifically regulated by law, as is the case with security guards. Any other form of outsourcing must be harshly reprimanded in the legal field.

It is therefore necessary for legislators not to remain inert, ignoring this situation. What is more, bills have been going through Congress for many years, such as Bill 4.330/2004, without a definitive solution.

It is clear that, despite the pressure of unemployment and private enterprise's constant quest for profit, the labor inspectorate and the labor courts are working hard to preserve workers' rights. In view of this, it must be said that the judiciary must be called upon by employees in order to curb the abuses of employers.

All of this is aimed at preserving the dignity of the worker and the social values of work, as presuppositions of the 1988 Federal Constitution. It is the responsibility of society, companies and workers to ensure that labor rights are enforced, not ignoring irregular situations, and always fighting for the reason and consequence of law and justice.

As far as Bill 4.330/2004 is concerned, it regulates outsourcing in Brazil, with the aim of making it legal and establishing the necessary parameters for its practice. Even in the face of some flaws, according to some jurists, there has been a clear evolution with the absorption of new forms of labor contracting, which ended up being perfected by Sumula 331 of the TST, which standardized the understanding of outsourcing, accepting the lawful supply of labor, when the existence of a relationship of personality and direct subordination between the service taker and the outsourced employee is not configured.

A brief study of Bill No. 4.330/20045 allows us to infer that this bill promotes a radical paradigm shift in labor law, especially because of the possibility it opens up for the company's core business to be the subject of a contract between the contracting company and the service provider. This project is causing a great deal of concern because of the uncertainties it brings, especially with regard to labor relations.

Great care must be taken to ensure that companies benefit to the detriment of the loss of rights acquired by workers throughout history. It is necessary to seek and maintain a balance between employer/employee relations. The danger lies in the fact that companies operating at a national level will certainly be able to use outsourced labor, with wage reductions and a reduction in labor charges, which will immediately lead to layoffs, and then the leveling of wages through the floor applicable to service providers, which, as we know, are practically derisory in relation to other categories of workers.

So, on the one hand, outsourcing brings benefits and advantages to organizations, but, on the other hand, there needs to be strict legislation that doesn't allow companies to commit injustices against their workers. Sumula 331 of the Superior Labor Court has been effective on the issue of outsourcing in Brazil.

REFERENCES

AMERICO, Pla Rodrigues. **The principles of labor law**. LTr, 2004.

AMERICO, Pla Rodrigues. **The principles of labor law**. LTr, 2004.

AMERICO, Pla Rodrigues. **The principles of labor law**. LTr, 2004.

ASSOCIAÇÃO BRASILEIRA DE NORMAS TECNICAS. **NBR 14724:** information and documentation: academic papers: presentation. Rio de Janeiro, 2011.

BARROS, Alice Monteiro de. **Labor Law Course.** 3ª ed. rev. e ampl. Sao Paulo: LTr, 2010.

BASILE, Cesar Reinaldo. **Labor Law**. 4th edition. Sao Paulo. Saraiva. 2011.

BARROS, Alice Monteiro. Salary Isonomy. **Journal of the National Academy of Labor Law**. Year VII, No. 7, Sao Paulo: LTr, 1999.

BOBBIO, Noberto. **The Age of Rights**. Rio de Janeiro, Editora Campos, 1992

BONAVIDES, Paulo. **Constitutional Law Course.** Sao Paulo. Malheiros. 2014.

BRAZIL, **Civil Code**. Ordinary Law No. 10.406, of January 10, 2002.

BRAZIL, **Consolidation of Labor Laws**. Decree-Law No. 5,452, of May 1, 1943.

BRAZIL, **Constitution of the Federative Republic of Brazil**: promulgated on October 5, 1988.

BRAZIL, **Law 6.019** of January 3, 1974. Provides for temporary work in urban companies, and other measures.

BRAZIL, **Law 7.102** of June 20, 1983. Provides for security for financial establishments, establishes rules for the constitution and operation of private companies that operate security and cash transportation services, and makes other provisions.

BRAZIL, **Law 8.666** of June 21, 1993. Regulates article 37, item XXI, of the Constitution, establishes rules for public administration bids and contracts, and makes other provisions.

BRAZIL, **Law 8.949** of December 9, 1994. Adds a paragraph to art. 442 of the Consolidation of Labor Laws (CLT) to declare that there is no employment relationship between cooperatives and their members.

BRAZIL, **Law 9.472** of July 16, 1997. Provides for the organization of telecommunications services, the creation and operation of a regulatory body and other institutional aspects, under the terms of Constitutional Amendment No. 8 of 1995.

BRAZIL, **Law 9.601** of January 21, 1998. Provides for fixed-term employment contracts and other measures.

BRASIL, **Sumula 51** TST.

BRAZIL, **Sumula 256** TST.

BRAZIL, **Sumula 331** TST.

BULOS, U. L. **Constitutional Law Course.** Ed. Saraiva. S. Paulo. 2011

CASSAR, Volia Bomfim. **Labor Law.** Sao Paulo. Metodo. 2015.

CATHARINO, Jose Martins. **Neoliberalism and its aftermath: privatization, deregulation, flexibilization, outsourcing.** Sao Paulo: Ltr, 1997.

CATHARINO, Patricia. **Financial institutions and outsourcing**. Sao Paulo: Textonovo, 2005.

CAVALCANTE JUNIOR, Ophir. **The outsourcing of labor relations**. Sao Paulo: LTr, 1996.

CHAHAD, JOSE PAULO Z.; CACCIAMALI, MARIA CRISTINA. **Labor Market in Brazil: new labor practices, collective bargaining and fundamental rights at work.** Sao Paulo: Ltr, June 2003. .

CHERCHGLIA, Mariangela Leal. **Outsourcing of work in health services: some conceptual, legal and pragmatic aspects**. 2002. Available at: <http://www.opas.org.br/rh/publicacoes/textos_apoio/pub04U3T5.pdf>. Accessed on: Aug. 15, 2016.

COMPARATO, Fabio Konder. **A afirmação histórica dos direitos humanos**. 2. ed. rev. e ampl. Sao Paulo: Saraiva. 2001.

CORDEIRO, Karine da Silva. **Social Fundamental Rights:** Dignity of the Human Person and Existential Minimum, The Role of the Judiciary, Porto Alegre, Livraria do Advogado Editora, 2012.

CUNHA, Alexandre dos Santos. **The normativity of the human person:** the legal study of personality and the 2002 Civil Code. Sao Paulo. Saraiva. 2008.

CURY, Munir; SILVA, Antonio Fernando do Amaral; MENDEZ, Emilio Garcia. **Estatuto da criança e do adolescente comentado**. 3. ed. Sao Paulo: Malheiros Editores, 2010.

DELGADO, Mauricio Godinho. **Labor Law Course**. 7ª ed. Sao Paulo: LTr, 2008. 432-433 p., citing: A socio-political analysis of outsourcing in the Brazilian labor market can be found in MARTINS, Heloisa de Souza and RAMALHO, Jose Ricardo. "Outsourcing - Diversity and Negotiation in the World of Work". Sao Paulo: HUCITEC/CEDI/NETS, 1994.

DELGADO, Mauricio Godinho. **Labor Law Course**. Sao Paulo. LTr. 2009

. **Course in Labor Law**. 2nd ed. Sao Paulo: LTr, 1999.

Labor Law Course. 7th ed. Sao Paulo: LTr, 2008.

Labor Law Course, Sao Paulo, LTr. Editora LTDA. 2011.

FACHIN, O. **Fundamentos de metodologia**. 4. ed. Sao Paulo: Saraiva, 2003.

GARCIA, Gustavo Filipe Barbosa, **Curso de Direito do Trabalho**. 2nd ed. Sao Paulo: Metodo, 2008.

GARCIA, Gustavo Filipe Barbosa. **Labor Law Course**. 2nd ed. Sao Paulo: Metodo, 2008.

GIL, Antonio Carlos. **How to design research projects**. 4aed. Sao Paulo: Atlas, 2007.

GIOSA, Livio Antonio. **Outsourcing: a strategic approach.** 5th ed. rev. and expanded. Sao Paulo: Pioneira Thomson Learning, 2003.

Outsourcing: a strategic approach. 5. ed. Sao Paulo: Pioneira, 2010.

IBRHAHIM ISKANDAR, Jamil. **ABNT standards:** commented for scientific papers. 3. ed. revised and updated. Curitiba: Jurua, 2008.

JOHNSTON, Aldem. **A study of the principles of labor law**. 15 Jan 2002. Available at: http://www.direitonet.com.br/artigos/exibir/543/Um-estudo- about-the-principles-of-labor-law. Accessed on September 15, 2016.

LAKATOS, E. M; MARCONI, M. A. **Fundamentals of Scientific Methodology.** 6aed. Sao Paulo: Atlas, 2006.

MARCONI, M.; LAKATOS, E. M. **Tecnicas de Pesquisa**. 4 ed, Sao Paulo: Atlas, 1999.

MARTINS, Sergio Pinto. **Outsourcing and labor law.** Sao Paulo. Atlas. 2012.

MARTINS, Sergio Pinto. **Outsourcing and Labor Law**. 6th ed. Sao Paulo: Atlas, 2003.

MARTINS, Sergio Pinto. **Labor Law.** 21st ed. Sao Paulo: Atlas, 2008.

MELO, Mauricio Correia de. Labor Prosecutor. **Outsourcing.** Sao Paulo. Forum Magazine (2010). Available at: <http://www.revistaforum.com.br>. Accessed on: September 3, 2016.

MONTAL, Zelia Maria Cardoso; GAMBA, Juliane Caravieri Martins. **The Human Right to Adequate Food:** revisiting the thought of Josue de Castro. Revista Juridica da Presidencia. Brasilia, vol. 12, no. 95, Oct/Jan, 2009/2010.

MORAES, Alexandre de. **Constituigao do Brasil interpretada e legislagao constitucional**. Sao Paulo: Atlas, 2007.

. **Brazil's Constitution Interpreted**. Sao Paulo, Editora Atlas, 2003.

MORAES, Paulo Douglas Almeida de. **Indirect contracting and outsourcing of services in the core business of legal entities**: legal possibility and social convenience. 2003.
Available at: <www.mte.gov.br/delegacias/ms/ms_monografia.pdf>. Accessed on: 09 Sep. 2016.

NBR 6023: **information and documentation: references: preparation.** Rio de Janeiro, 2002.

NBR 10520: **information and documentation: citations in documents: presentation.** Rio de Janeiro, 2002.

OLIVEIRA, Umberto Machado de. **Constitutional principles of agrarian law**. In:. Curitiba: Jurua, 2003.

OLIVEIRA, Marcelo Augusto Souto de. **Outsourcing:** Forward or Backward? Sao Paulo. Saraiva. 2012. Available at: http://www.ibcbrasil.com.br. Accessed on: September 15, 2016.

PASTORE, Jose; PASTORE, Jose Eduardo. **Outsourcing.** Sao Paulo. LTR. 2015.

PAULO, Vicente; ALEXANDRINO, Marcelo. **Constitutional Law.** Sao Paulo. Metodo 8ª ed. 2014.

PIRES, Aurelio. **Outsourcing:** responsibilities - a topic for reflection. Labor Supplement. Sao Paulo. LTrn. 31, 2011.

QUEIROZ, Carlos Alberto Ramos Soares de. **Manual e terceirização**. 9. ed. Sao Paulo: STS. 2010.

ROBORTELLA, Luiz Carlos Amorim. **Modern labor law.** Sao Paulo. LTr. 2010.

ROCHA, Maria Fadua Lima. SANTIAGO, Nestor Eduardo Araruna. **Tax crimes, installment payments and extinguishment of punishability: an** attack on the Federal Constitution? Sao Paulo. Scientia Magazine. 2012.

RODRIGUES, Rosualdo and TURCATO, Sandra. Outsourcing erodes the labor market. **Anamatra Magazine**. Ano XIX, n° 56, Brasilia: Publication of the National Association of Magistrates of the Labor Court, January 2009.

SARLET, Ingo Wolfgang. **Dignity of the Human Person and Fundamental Rights in the Federal Constitution of 1988.** 5. ed. Porto Alegre: Livraria do Advogado, 2007.

SEVERINO, Antonio Joaquim. **Metodologia do trabalho cientifico.** 21. ed. rev. e ampl. Sao Paulo: Cortez, 2002.

SILVA, Jose Afonso da. **Course in Positive Constitutional Law.** Sao Paulo. Malheiros Editores. 2010.

SUSSEKIND, Arnaldo. New regulations on temporary work and outsourcing of services. **Consulex Legal Magazine**. Year V, No. 109, Brasilia: Consulex Publishing House. 2001.

MIX
Papier aus verantwortungsvollen Quellen
Paper from responsible sources
FSC® C105338

Printed by Books on Demand GmbH, Norderstedt / Germany